THE PHANTOM ARM

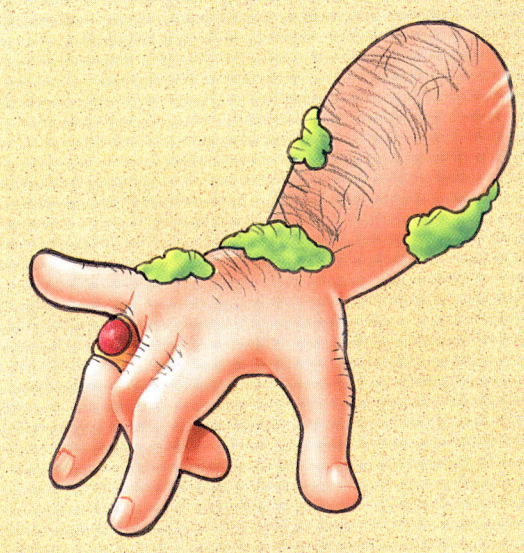

Written by Carol Krueger
Illustrated by Damon J. Taylor

Inheriting a Pile of Trouble

I'll never forget that day. That was the day it all started. William and I had just gotten home from school, and Mom had this strange look on her face.

"What's wrong, Mom?"

"We're going to move," she answered.

"Not again!" yelled William. "We've moved twice this year!"

Our Dad doesn't live with us, and we always seem to be moving.

"Can I go and live with Dad?" I asked.

"No, you're living with me—in Uncle Tiberius's old house."

William's eyes and mouth popped open. A shiver flickered down my back.

"You're kidding!" I said.

"No, I'm not, Jamie," Mom said with a nervous look. "You know Uncle Tiberius died last week. Well, today his lawyer came to see me. It seems I'm his last living relative."

"So he willed his moldy old mansion to you?" William rolled his eyes dramatically.

"Yes," said Mom.

Nobody said anything, and I tried to think of Uncle Tiberius. I'd only seen him maybe three times. He was very old when I was little. He had a stubby beard and hardly any hair on his head. He also smelled funny. Uncle Tiberius had been a famous scientist. He worked at a hospital, and he used to bring strange things home.

"Mom, we CAN'T live there!" I cried.

"None of my friends will ever come over!" William groaned.

"Well, we've run out of money for the rent on this place. We can live in Uncle Tiberius's house or in a tent on Grandma's lawn!"

"The tent," William and I said together.

But Mom was determined. We had to go.

We spent the next week packing our things, and on Sunday everything got loaded onto the truck owned by Mom's boss, Tony. Uncle Tiberius lived by the sea. The road was narrow and wound up a steep hill. It was going to take forever to bike to our school!

I sat in the truck and looked at the house. It was a huge, brick, three-story building with a tower right at the top. Ivy clung to most of the front, and the windows were small and cramped. Weeds grew everywhere. I could hear the sea behind the house.

"Well, just think—we each can have our own floor!" laughed Mom. She was quite excited and was the first out of the truck.

The front door opened, and an elderly woman stepped onto the porch.

"Oh, I forgot to tell you," said Mom. "A cat and a housekeeper come with the house."

"Come on in!" The woman smiled as she walked down the steps. I wanted to run.

"Here, take this, Jamie," said Mom as she handed me a stool.

I trudged slowly up the stone path—past the endless weeds choking the wild roses, past the birdbath with muddy water, and past the granite lions guarding the front porch.

I tripped going through the front door and sprawled on the hall floor. A small motor purred in my right ear, and I felt fluff against my mouth. Something wet touched my face. I opened my eyes and saw a black cat's nose.

"Snore!" cried the woman. "That's no way to greet the new owners of the house!"

Mom helped me up, and I sat on the stool. Snore was a huge black-and-white cat. He was so round, he looked like a furry balloon. He jumped right up onto my lap and started gently digging his toes into my jeans. I'm not very fond of cats. Our last cat scratched apart my school jacket.

The housekeeper introduced herself. Her name was Mabel Martinelli.

Mom, William, Tony, and I carried in our few pieces of furniture. With our things unloaded, Tony muttered a good-bye and drove off in the empty truck. I felt as if he were the last contact with the ordinary world.

It was sad to think that after all these years we owned so little. It didn't seem to matter much though because Uncle Tiberius had rooms of furniture. It was moldy and old—like the house. The carpet smelled real funny. It was a horrible dark pattern, and the walls had an even darker wood paneling.

"I'll show you around," said Mabel.

She showed us through room after room of musty furniture and velvet drapes. The only part of the house I even faintly liked was the big old wooden staircase; it curved up to each floor.

Snore followed us everywhere. I could see why he was called Snore. He purred so loudly that he sounded just like someone snoring.

"Can we see the tower room?" asked Mom as we stood on the second-floor landing.

Mabel's face turned pale. "You must never go to the tower room!" she proclaimed in a strange voice.

"Why?"

"I can't tell you, but you must promise me—never EVER go into the tower room!"

"Why can't we go into the tower room?" I asked.

With a long pause and a long stare, Mabel said solemnly, "That was your uncle's SPECIAL place. That's where he conducted some of his top-secret scientific experiments."

"Now that he has died, shouldn't we clean it out?" asked Mom.

"Oh, no!" cried Mabel, standing firmly by the stairway. "He gave strict instructions that the room must be kept locked and never EVER opened!"

Mom shook her head and made that funny noise she always makes with her tongue.

"Sounds a bit odd to me," she murmured.

We all walked downstairs.

The Forbidden Room

My room was on the second floor. It was at the back of the house and looked out over the sea. I'd never had a room like it. It was as big as our old living room. It had a high ceiling with all this patterned stuff on it. The light bulb at the end of a long cord was covered by a curly pink glass shade. The closet was as big as a hallway. It was a shame I didn't have the clothes to fill it.

Snore really seemed to like me. He jumped on the bed that was in the center of the room. He made that funny noise and pushed his white paws up and down on the pink quilt.

Just my luck, I thought. He'll probably shed all over it.

I didn't have the heart to tell Snore I really didn't like him.

Mom left me so that I could unpack my things. My old teddy bear that Dad gave me when I was four took its place on my bed. This bed was much bigger than any of the beds I'd ever had before. The bear looked lost, even with Snore curled up beside it. I opened the window to let fresh air in. I hated the musty smell. I don't think anyone had slept in that room for years.

That night I noticed that Mabel had put on clean sheets. They were white and stiff and didn't fold around my face like our own sheets. I slept well that night. It was kind of nice to hear the soft roar of the sea—almost soothing. For what was ahead of me, boy, did I need something soothing!

Uncle Tiberius had left Mom his car as well as the house. Mom was really excited about that. She hadn't had a car in years. We were creatures of buses and trains. William and I weren't so thrilled about the car. It was old like the house—REAL old. It was black and had a funny shape.

"Mom, you can't drive us to school in THAT!" cried William.

"Well, I have to show you the way the first morning. You can ride your bikes tomorrow."

"If we get up at five o'clock…" I groaned.

After breakfast Mom drove us in the old car. It made funny noises on the way. William was desperately hoping that it wouldn't get there. But it did, and Mom stopped in front of the school.

"I'll pick you up at three," she said and then left us on the pavement as she rumbled off with a loud roar and wheeze.

Boy, that was embarrassing. Every kid in the school must have seen us.

"Are you sure it can't get any louder!" they yelled.

My friend Angela kept asking me all these questions about the house—and there was worse to come! Our teacher, Ms. Fong, made me stand up in front of the class and tell the other students about our new home. How much can a kid take! I left out the bit about the tower room.

"Your uncle was an extremely interesting man," Ms. Fong told me. "And quite famous. He did a lot of special research for the hospital."

Why did I have to have a famous uncle? I would have preferred a nice, ordinary one.

After school Angela talked me into letting her come home with me. "My mom can come and pick me up afterward," she argued.

I didn't really want Angela to see where I lived. "It's too far!" I said.

"Oh, Mom won't mind," Angela replied as her mom's car came into view.

"Your mom might not say yes," I countered hopefully.

But she did. She wrote down our address and waved good-bye as we got into that awful black car. Mom revved it up extra hard, and we drove off in a cloud of blue smoke. I think she did it on purpose. She really liked that car.

When Angela saw the house, she gave a little gasp. "It really does look spooky!"

I showed her all the rooms, and then we came to the tower. "What's up those small stairs?" she asked.

"That's the tower room," I said. "THAT was my uncle's special laboratory."

"Well, let's go," Angela suggested.

"No, we can't."

"Why not?"

"It's a special, secret room," I explained. "No one's allowed in there EVER!"

"Oh, come on, Jamie!" Angela whined in that pleading little voice of hers. "One little peek wouldn't hurt."

"Yes, it would!" said William, who had just joined us.

"Oh, come on, William. Spoilsport!" Angela taunted him. "What would one little look do?"

"I don't know, but we are NOT allowed to!" hissed William.

"I'll give you SIX of my baseball cards if you do." Angela raised her eyebrows at him.

That was too much for William. His eyes sort of gleamed. "Did you say SIX?"

"Yes, I'll give you SIX of them!"

That did it. William climbed up the narrow steps and put his hand on the doorknob.

The Tower's Secret

The door wouldn't open.

"It's locked!" said William.

I could see the disappointment in Angela's eyes. I was quite relieved. "There, see, we aren't supposed to go in there!"

Angela wouldn't let it rest. "There must be a key somewhere!"

"I don't know where it is," I said.

"But SOMEONE must have it. After all, it's a door, and it's got a keyhole," insisted Angela, looking at the old wooden door.

"If I find the key, will you give me EIGHT cards?" William asked her.

"No!" I interrupted. "We've gone far enough already. We shouldn't even be standing here!"

"What could happen? Are you scared your uncle's ghost is going to rush out and scare us to death?" sneered Angela.

"No," I said.

"Well, don't be a pain, Jamie. Let's find the key."

I stood firm on the stairs. "No. I'm NOT going to take part in this."

"William, I'll give you TEN cards if you can find the key!" said Angela, her eyes suddenly flashing.

That did it. William sprang into action. He started looking in cabinets, on top of doorways, and even under mats. I just followed them around hopelessly. I kept thinking I really should tell Mom.

"Where would the keys be kept?" asked William.

"Doesn't Mabel have a set of keys in the kitchen somewhere?" suggested Angela.

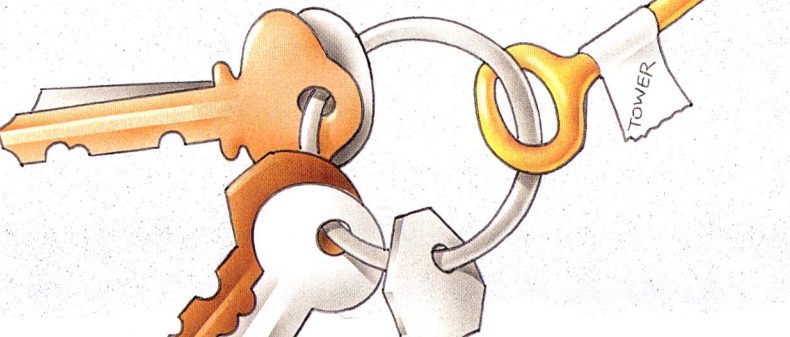

My heart dropped. I had seen a bunch of keys in the kitchen and so had William. He was down the stairs in a flash. In the kitchen I could smell a roast in the oven and heard Mom and Mabel in the next room.

"Don't do it!" I said in a loud whisper.

But Angela seized the large bunch of keys hanging on a peg.

"Got them!" she hissed.

By this time William had cold feet. "Maybe we shouldn't do it!" he said in an uneasy voice.

"I definitely don't think we should!" I said firmly.

But Angela wouldn't be stopped. "What's wrong with you? Killjoy!"

"I don't want the cards anymore," said William. "Put the keys back, Angela."

Instead, Angela raced out of the kitchen and up the stairs.

"What are we going to do?" William asked me. "I'm going to tell Mom."

"No, let's wrestle the keys away from her," I replied.

We bolted out of the kitchen. I tripped over Snore again, but he didn't seem to mind. Angela stood at the top of the stairs with a triumphant look on her face.

"I've got it! It's got 'Tower' written on it!"

"ANGELA! NO!" we cried.

Up the narrow stairs we went, but we were too late. Angela had turned the key in the lock.

Slowly the door opened.

15

I just stood there paralyzed. I waited for lightning to strike or for the earth to open up. Neither happened. Instead, Angela disappeared into the room. There was dead silence. A strange smell wafted into the hall. It was like nothing I'd ever smelled before. William and I just stood there. Neither of us moved. After what seemed like an eternity, Angela came out.

"You should see what's in there!"

"I don't want to," muttered William.

"I'm not going in there," I said. "Come on, Angela, you've had your look. Now close the door!"

"But you should SEE what's in there!" she exclaimed.

"Angela! Close the door!"

"But you should see it!" she cried again. "There's this glass case, and inside is an arm!"

We froze.

"An ARM???"

"Yes, an arm! A HUMAN arm with a hand. It's a hairy hand with yellow fingernails, and there's this red ring on one of the fingers."

William and I were too scared to say anything.

"Come and have a look!" said Angela. "It's really freaky!"

I couldn't help myself. I had to see it. I went in. There it was: this spooky arm in a glass case. I couldn't believe it was real. I went over to the case and slid my fingers over the glass. And that's when it happened. My thumb accidentally released the catch.

All of a sudden, the strong hairy arm sprang to life and flung itself to the floor. Smelly, thick green ooze dribbled out. The arm scampered across the floor and out the door!

Chasing a Runaway Arm

I was so frightened. I actually felt as if I might be sick. Angela had turned a strange color, and she wasn't smiling any more.

"What do we do now?" she squealed in a high-pitched voice.

"What do WE do? You mean what do YOU do. YOU opened the door!" William replied angrily.

My first thought was to catch the arm. But we watched as it opened the hall window and crawled outside. I raced to the window and took a deep breath. No way was I going to hang my head out the window if a hand was going to yank it off my shoulders. Through the glass I could see it scurry down the bricks like some horrible furry snake. It got to the drainpipe, then disappeared around the side of the house.

"What's the matter?" Mom and Mabel came running upstairs.

"Oh, nothing!" said Angela in the same silly, high-pitched voice.

"We heard someone scream!"

That's when I remembered that I'd screamed really loud when I saw the arm. Then Mabel noticed the door.

"You've opened the door!" she whispered.

"Angela did it!" said William.

"I didn't mean any harm!" cried Angela.

"You didn't mean any harm! Do you know what you've done?" Mabel was yelling now.

"Yes," said Angela. "This creepy hand escaped from the case and disappeared out the window."

Mabel's face drained, losing what little color it had. She sighed and then said, "We must find it at once! It must be returned to the case and locked up again. We have to find it. Something terrible will happen if we don't!"

"Mabel, arms don't walk by themselves. Even LEGS don't walk on their own!" said Mom in her usual matter-of-fact tone.

Mabel didn't seem to hear. "Someone could die unless we find that arm!"

I don't know whether it was shock or the tone of Mabel's voice that made Mom move, but move she did.

"Well, let's look for the thing," she insisted.

We followed her outside. I was really scared now. What if I did catch this thing—was it going to kill me?

We stayed together. At least there was safety in numbers. We searched the weedy garden. We went around the back, past the unmowed lawn, past the toolshed. That's when I saw it. The creepy hand was coming around the corner of the toolshed door.

"It's in there—in the toolshed!" I yelled.

Mabel stopped. "Don't go near it!" she screamed.

"You told us to catch it!"

"Just stand back!" she cried.

Frightened, we stood together by the side of the house. Soon the hand came out and crept quickly across the grass.

"Catch it now while you can!" shrieked Mabel.

We raced after it, but it was crafty. It sped quickly through the grass and through the weeds, losing itself in tangles of dandelion.

Mabel was determined to catch it. She ran ahead of us, slashing the weeds. Then we saw her grab hold of it. She screamed as it pulled her down the path. On it went, its spooky fingers pulling Mabel's hand.

We watched in horror as the hand pulled Mabel toward our car. None of us could think of what to do.

Suddenly it stopped. It seemed to see an elderly couple, who were just getting into their car down the road.

Quick as a flash, the hand let go of Mabel and crawled like a giant spider over the blacktop and up onto the bumper of the other car—just as the car took off down the road.

Mabel was in a state of shock. Her breathing was funny, and she fainted, falling to the ground. We all carried her inside. Even though she was small and thin, we still had a hard time getting her up the path. By the time we got her into the hall chair, she was just starting to come to.

"My heart pills are on the kitchen shelf," she mumbled. I went into the kitchen while the others stayed with her. I found a little bottle of red pills with "M. Martinelli" typed on the label.

I quickly filled a glass of water and went back to the front hall. Mabel was going on and on. Mom kept telling her to relax and take deep breaths. Mom always says that whenever anybody is upset.

I gave Mabel the bottle of pills and the glass of water. She swallowed one with a big gulp of water. Her face relaxed a bit. "We'll never get it now. Goodness knows what harm it will do!"

"What do you mean?" Mom asked her. "How do you know it's dangerous?"

Mabel said quietly, "Because that's the arm of a murderer!"

A Murderous Arm

There were about three seconds of silence, and then we all cried at once, "A MURDERER!!!"

Mabel was breathing normally now, but she was about the only one who was. Even Mom was scared now. "Listen, arms can't move by themselves," she said after a while. "There must be some logical explanation."

"Maybe it's got batteries!" said William suddenly.

"I don't think so," murmured Mabel. "I know it doesn't SEEM possible, but, with your uncle, a lot of strange things happened."

"I'm really sorry!" howled Angela.

She was crying now. I'd never seen Angela cry. Even when her finger got slammed in the door, she only squealed once. But actually, none of us felt very sorry for her as the tears rolled down her cheeks from red, swimming eyes.

"We told you not to open that door!" snorted William. I was going to remind him that he was all for it when ten baseball cards were at stake, but I decided not to make things worse.

"I think the only thing we can do is go back up to the laboratory and go over some of the professor's notes. That might help us," remarked Mabel, who had become surprisingly calm.

22

We followed her up the stairs, then climbed the narrow steps to the tower room. I felt as if I were walking into an Egyptian tomb. I kept imagining that the roof was going to fall onto my head or that my uncle's notebook was going to come flying out in my face. I even imagined Uncle Tiberius materializing through the wall to tell us off.

None of these things happened, of course. The room was just as he had left it. There were no cobwebs, not even any spiders on the slanted ceiling. But there were books and strange instruments everywhere. The empty glass case stood as a reminder of our previous visit. Strange, slimy green liquid was smeared across the floor.

"How do you know the arm was from a murderer?" William asked Mabel.

"Tiberius told me," she replied

"He did?" William questioned.

"Yes. We were having breakfast one day, and he just told me. It was after I read about a murder in the morning paper. The police were going to arrest the murderer, but he died in a car crash."

"I remember!" said Mom. "The Fernandez-Fox case. Anton Hall was the murderer."

I shivered. I remembered the kids talking about it at school. We'd heard about Anton Hall's house being for sale and no one wanting to buy it!

"What was Uncle Tiberius doing with his arm?" William wondered.

"Well, that's what I don't know," said Mabel. "He just said that he was carrying out a scientific experiment on it. Something about studying a person's character through the lines of his palm. But he never really told me. He only warned me NEVER to go into the laboratory and to make sure that it always stayed locked."

Mom was looking at some of his books. "There's a list here in this book. It's got the date he received the arm from the hospital."

"Maybe we should call the hospital and tell them everything," Angela suggested. That was her first good idea of the day.

25

A phone was on the desk underneath a bunch of papers. Mabel dug it out, and Mom showed her the hospital phone number in the book.

Mabel dialed the number, and we all waited. We could hear it ringing inside the receiver. When someone answered, Mabel said, "Hello. May I speak with Dr. Patel, please?"

There was another long pause.

"Hello, this is Mabel Martinelli, Professor Tiberius Taylor's housekeeper... Yes, I know he passed away last week, but we have a problem. He received an arm from you a while ago... Yes, the arm of Anton Hall... Well, he kept it in a glass case, and now it's missing. It escaped and crawled away... What do you mean, am I crazy? Of course not! I tell you this arm crawled over the lawn... Hello?"

She put the phone down. "He hung up!"

"It DOES sound crazy!" said Mom.

"Maybe you should call the TV station. They might want to do a feature on the whole thing and call it 'The Phantom Arm,'" William suggested.

That actually wasn't such a bad idea. Maybe then people would call the station if they saw the arm.

"Well, I'm not calling," said Mabel. She sat down on a wooden stool. "I don't think anyone will believe us. I mean, we can hardly call the police and report a missing arm, last seen wearing a ring and heading north!"

"There's a newspaper article here about the Fernandez-Fox case," said Mom. "It took place in Rosedale."

"Maybe the arm's trying to return to the scene of the crime!" I yelled.

"The article doesn't say exactly where the murder happened," said Mom. "It could have been anywhere in town. We're looking for a needle in a haystack."

Mabel sighed, "Tomorrow we'll go to the police and see if we can find the address where the murder took place. It's too dark. We'll never find the arm now."

We locked up the laboratory, and Angela's mom came to pick her up. I'd never seen Angela so quiet. Her mom kept asking what the matter was as they drove off. That night I lay in bed wondering—where was the arm, and what was it doing? I felt strangely hot. I thought of that hairy arm creeping… crawling… and CLUTCHING!

The Scene of the Crime

The next morning, I got up really early. I'd hardly slept. We all got into that horrible black car, and Mabel sped down the hill. I'd planned to ride my bike to school, but there was no way I was biking with that arm on the loose! I didn't even care if people saw us in the car. It didn't seem to matter.

We arrived at the Rosedale police station an hour before school started. No one was at the desk, so we pushed a little white button. A bell rang somewhere on the other side of the wall. An officer came out. "Can I help you?"

"We wondered if you could tell us where the Fernandez-Fox case took place," Mabel inquired calmly.

"Are you tourists or something?" asked the officer.

"No, we're doing a special project about the case," replied Mom. "We've read a lot about it, and we'd like to see where the murder actually happened."

The officer looked at us for a few seconds. Then he said, "I can't give you the exact address. That information is confidential. You could ask the locals. I think it was around George Street."

By the time Mabel had thanked him, we were in the car. It didn't take us long to find George Street.

I had this horrible feeling in my stomach. I wondered what we'd actually find. Mabel reasoned that if we could catch the arm and get it back to the hospital our problems would be over.

We stopped at the bottom of George Street. It was a steep, narrow street with old-fashioned wooden houses, all joined closely together. We saw some school kids walking down the street. They weren't kids from our school. I would have died of shame if they were. William hopped out of the car and asked them straight out, "Do you know where the Fernandez-Fox murder took place?"

"Yeah," said a boy, "the murder took place up the hill in that empty house—but don't go near it. It's haunted!"

I could see that they wanted to stay and talk about it, which wouldn't be a bad idea. It would be great if someone else had seen the arm. But Mom got out of the car, thanked them, and took us up the hill.

30

    I was mulling over in my mind what we were going to do if we found the arm. We couldn't exactly lasso it, and we couldn't put it in a net.

    We stopped in front of the empty house. A "For Sale" sign stood out front. The lawn was like a jungle, and the front windows were broken. It looked really spooky.

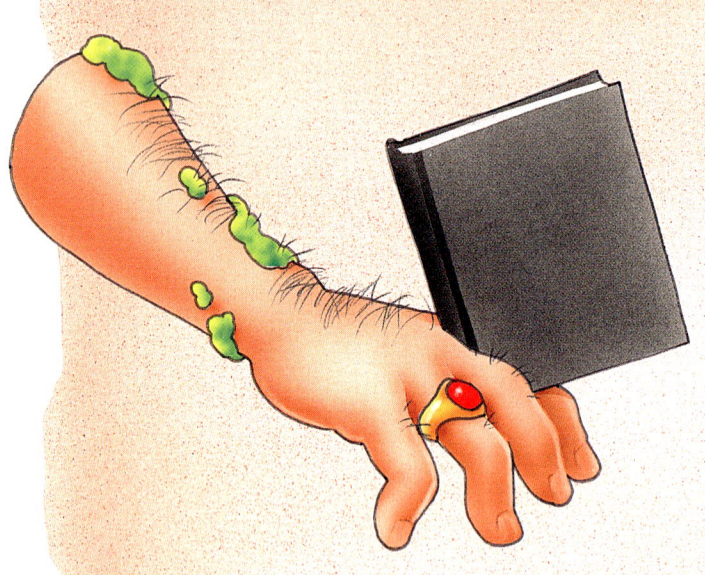

William yelled, "There it is! Look!"

We turned, and, sure enough, there it was! This horrible thing was crawling down the sidewalk. It had something in its fingers that looked like a book.

"After it!" I cried.

We raced down the hill. It must have seen us—if that's possible, since it didn't have any eyes. It seemed to sense that we were following it. It raced faster and faster away from us and around the corner. Breathlessly we reached the corner. The arm was nowhere in sight.

"It's gone," murmured William.

It was gone. It was nowhere to be seen. We stood waiting to see if it would come out of somewhere. But it didn't. We walked up and down, looking behind fences, but we couldn't find it.

"It's gotten away from us again!" Mabel cried.

"No use staying here," said Mom. "We'll drop you off at school. Then we'll come back and drive around the neighborhood."

This time Mom drove. She stopped down the street from the school. "Here you are. No one will see you get out of the car."

"It doesn't matter much now," I mumbled.

I walked up the steps and realized that I was about five minutes late. I noticed Angela's coat hook was empty. I hung up my backpack and wearily sat down at my desk. Angela's seat was empty.

"You're late," said Ms. Fong. As if I didn't know! I could see Jimmy Knight snickering. I wonder how he would feel if HE saw an arm run away!

32

The day went on as if nothing had ever happened. The only thing that was different was that Angela wasn't there. Angela was never absent.

I had lunch on my own, and then we had math. I wasn't in the mood for that. But something much worse was to follow. Just as I opened my pencil case, I saw it! The huge hairy arm crept over the windowsill right by my desk. It was inside the classroom, and it was heading straight for me!

From Hunter to Hunted

I could hear someone screaming, and I realized it was me. Then I could hear other screams. I stood up, and still the arm was coming toward me. It's fingers were curled, and they kept moving. Like spider legs, the fingers crawled quickly over my desk and onto my chair.

"Do something!" I yelled.

Ms. Fong came running and grabbed hold of the arm with both hands. With savage strength it squeezed her hand until she let go. Then it was after me again. It raced between the desks, past my horrified classmates. It chased me out of the classroom door.

Desperately I ran. I ran like I had never run before—across the playground and out the school gate. I kept looking behind me, and there it was—that horrible hairy arm and hand—still following me. I kept on running. I had jumbled thoughts as I ran. At least I would be believed, now that about thirty witnesses had seen the arm. But that seemed small comfort now that the arm was after ME!

I reached the stores. I could see people talking, pushing strollers, and looking at store displays. Obviously no one had noticed the hand because everything seemed normal. I felt a pain in my side, so I quickly stepped into an alley. The arm went past, searching for me.

I held my breath. I was trapped now. The alley was between two stores. There was no escape. If it came back for me, it would get me. I panted and waited. The arm didn't come around the corner, so I just stood there. I got my breath, and then I decided to make a run for it. Open space was safer than an alley. I looked out. I couldn't see the arm. It was almost with relief that I stepped out. Then I heard a loud toot. Ms. Fong was honking her car horn and waving her hand wildly.

"Get in!" she shouted.

I reached for the car door, but before I could open it, I saw the arm again. It scuttled around the side of the car. Its terrible fingers just missed my ankle as I ran on. On and on I kept running, and still the arm was following me!

I ran out of breath at the library. My face was hot, my side hurt, and I thought my lungs had turned inside out. The brick wall felt cool against my damp back as I leaned against it and sucked in buckets of air. The arm was nowhere to be seen! I closed my eyes and took in more air.

35

That's when I felt it—those strong fingers pulling my hair! The fingers had a tight grip on my hair. I screamed so loudly my ears rang.

Then I heard Mom's voice, "JAMIE!"

Mabel and Mom pulled up beside me and got out of the car. The fingers' grip tightened, and I felt a sharp yank on my hair. I yelled again, this time in pain. Then suddenly the fingers let go.

"Open the trunk!" Mabel screamed. They both struggled with the arm. I dashed to open the trunk. Mom and Mabel wrestled the arm inside and slammed the lid tight.

"Got it!" Mom cried triumphantly. Her face gleamed with relief. I could see the sweat on her forehead.

Mabel leaned against the car. "We've done it!" she declared. I was so relieved I did a stupid thing. I cried. I just couldn't help it. Sobs kept bubbling out of me.

Mom gave me a hug. "You were so brave, Jamie. What a terrible thing to happen!"

"What do we do now?" I sniffled when the sobs had finally stopped.

"I think we'd better take it to the hospital," said Mabel. "It's really their property. Uncle Tiberius certainly doesn't need it any more!"

We all thought that was a good idea.

Escaped... Again!

As we drove to the hospital, the hand began to tap inside the trunk. It was a slow knocking sound. "Mom, let's go—QUICKLY!"

Mom didn't waste any time. She parked at the hospital. I followed Mom and Mabel up the hospital steps to the front entrance.

"Please, could I see Dr. Patel? It's an emergency!" Mabel told a lady behind a desk.

"Hang on, I'll page him."

A little later a man with a thick black beard came through the doors.

"Dr. Patel, some people to see you." The receptionist pointed toward us.

"I'm Professor Tiberius Taylor's housekeeper. We spoke earlier today," said Mabel.

"Oh, yes. Really—" Dr. Patel started to say.

Mabel interrupted. "I've got something to show you. I'd like to return the arm that the professor was working on."

"You have it? Where is it?"

"In the car."

"Please, bring it in."

"Ummmm... Well... you'll need to help us," replied Mabel.

The doctor grumbled a bit, but he followed us out. When we got to the car, I stared, horrified. The trunk was open, and the arm was gone! A man was sitting on the pavement.

"I'm sorry," he said, getting up. "My car looks a little like this one. I must have been half asleep. I opened the trunk, and something jumped out and knocked me down."

The doctor looked puzzled. Mabel leaned against the car. I felt sick.

"The arm was in there," wailed Mabel. "I tried to explain this morning. I tell you, it moves!"

The doctor looked at the man. "Did YOU see a bodiless arm?"

38

"No, I didn't," he replied. "I didn't see anything. It happened so quickly. Sorry I can't be of more help." The man scurried toward another black car farther away.

"Well, if you haven't got the arm, I can't take it," said Dr. Patel. And he walked back toward the hospital.

"What do we do now?" cried Mom.

"We should go home," Mabel replied. "We've had enough for one day."

We drove home, and nobody said anything. Ms. Fong brought William home from school. She asked about the arm and promised she'd go down to the police station with us the next day. She muttered something else about how she'd never seen anything like it and then went home. At least somebody else was going to go to the police, but it didn't make me feel much better. I went to bed without eating much. I pulled the covers over my head and tried to sleep. The cool, salty air and the soft roar of the sea didn't help tonight.

Every night Snore did his paw thing on the quilt. He felt sort of nice on my feet, but the last few nights he'd been sleeping with William. I was pretty sure Snore was with William when I felt something on my quilt.

39

A Hand in the Night

I could feel it moving up the bed. There was the arm with those hideous fingers, crawling toward me!

I froze. It was as if time stood still. I must have screamed and jumped out of bed to open the door. Mom came rushing down the hall.

"It's after me again!" I screamed.

Mabel came running down the second flight of stairs. The hand was so close that its fingers snatched at the hem of my nightshirt. I ran so fast down the steps that I skipped about two at a time.

William came running from somewhere with a cat cage.

"See if we can catch it and put it in here!" he shrieked.

Mabel jumped onto the arm just as it was about to reach me. She wrestled with it. I stood there in terror, watching her roll on the floor with this ghastly, strong arm. Then Mom was on it with Mabel. The veins in Mom's neck bulged as she pulled and pulled the unwilling hand off Mabel and into the cage. It was in! Mom slammed the cage door, almost smashing the arm's thick fingers. She slammed the door closed and put in the pin to lock it.

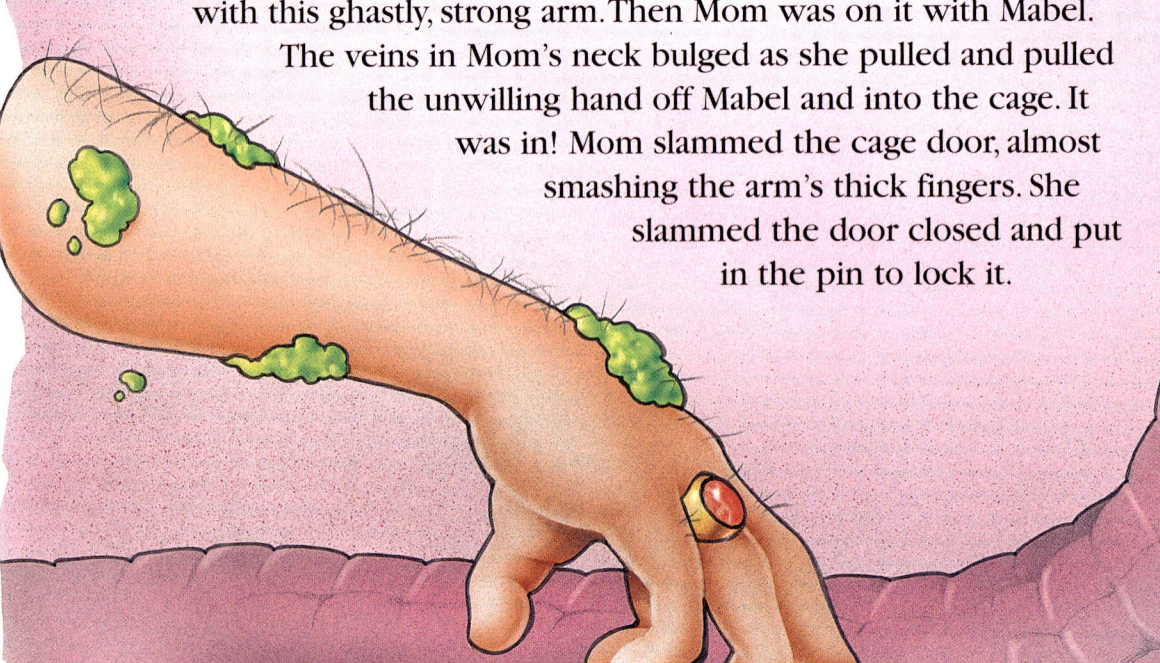

41

"You've caught it!" cried William.

I helped pick Mabel up off the floor. She was shaking as she pushed back the hair from her face. "Well, it can't do any harm in there!" she said. "I think we should take it back to the hospital."

"It's too late. Dr. Patel wouldn't be there," I said.

"Why don't we take it to the police," said William. For an eight-year-old kid, that was a pretty good suggestion.

We rushed to get dressed. Nobody said anything much. We all watched the arm in the cage. It didn't look so frightening now. It wasn't moving. It just looked like the hand of a dummy.

Soon we were ready to go. We went to the front door. I reached for the cage. Just then, I saw the fingers of the hand reach through the cage bars and remove the pin! The cage door swung open, and the hand leaped over the carpet toward me! I felt like I was in a play, doing the same scene over and over again. I ran for my life.

Outside on the lawn, I heard the others following behind. The hand was so fast I could feel it grabbing at my heels. I panted as I raced through the garden. Tall trees cast black shadows in the moonlight. I could hear Mabel's voice shouting, "STOP! STOP!"

42

I didn't know whether she was referring to me or the hand. I kept on blindly running and running, and then suddenly I felt nothing under me. Down I tumbled over the edge of a cliff. I screamed in terror as a mass of rocks and sea rolled before me.

A Helping Hand

Suddenly I slammed onto something rocky and hard, some sort of cliff shelf. The moon was full and high. The huge, dark cliff loomed above me. Down below I could see the sea—far, far below. My leg hurt really badly. I thought, I'll never get out of this!

I heard voices far above. "Jamie! Stay there! Don't move! We've called an ambulance. They'll be here soon!"

I just lay there, not hoping for anything. And then I heard it—a scratching sound. No, it was a crawling sound. Something was crawling down the cliff face. Something was crawling toward me—the ARM! By now I didn't care. I really didn't care. I just lay there, stiff as a board.

Then this soft hand reached for mine. It was so gentle that I let it take my hand. I felt a great strength. Suddenly the hand was like a vice grip, and I felt myself being pulled up—up, up it took me, up off the cliff shelf and onto the grassy top of the cliff. It had unbelievable strength.

There was a strange silence as I saw the others standing over me with astonished faces. Then the hand became gentle and soft again. It patted mine as if it were saying, "Don't be afraid of me." It held my hand and then shook it. It was a warm handshake, and although the arm was silent, it said louder than any words, "Thank you."

Then the arm crawled off into the darkness.

We couldn't believe the whole thing. It was gone. Not just the hand, the fear was gone too.

45

In the morning two police officers and Dr. Patel came by. One of the police officers was the man I'd seen the day before.

"The hand's gone," said Mom.

"We thought you might be interested in something," said one of the officers. "We found this book on my desk yesterday. Do you know whose it is?"

I looked at the black book. I remembered the arm carrying something the day before. It looked like a diary.

"No," I replied.

"It's the diary of Jim Spencer, the real murderer in the Fernandez-Fox case."

"But what about Anton Hall?" I asked the officer.

"When I read this, I discovered how Jim Spencer framed him. Jim Spencer was the real killer all the time. The diary proves that. Jim Spencer did it."

"Where is Spencer now?" asked Mom.

"He died in the same car crash that Anton Hall died in," the police officer replied.

I couldn't believe what I was hearing. It was now all starting to make sense. "So Anton's hand put the diary on your desk. He was trying to THANK me for giving him the chance to prove that he was not the guilty one!" I exclaimed.

Everyone looked at me.

"We found this note in the diary. We think it's for you," said the officer.

It read:

> Thanks for letting me out of the case so I could prove my innocence.

"Do you know where the hand is now?" asked Dr. Patel.

"It's gone," I said.

We told him about my fall over the cliff.

"I can't believe it happened," Mom murmured. "I've never heard of arms moving on their own."

"Nor have I," remarked Dr. Patel. "It's the strangest thing I've ever heard."

"It sounds like a horror movie!" cried William.

After that, things were pretty peaceful around the place. We never saw the arm again. We still don't know how it moved by itself either. I guess there are some things we'll never know!